LIE
DETECTOR
Oceans

WRITTEN BY
Simon Holland

ILLUSTRATED BY
Lee Cosgrove

PICTURE WINDOW BOOKS
a capstone imprint

Picture Window Books are published by
Capstone, 1710 Roe Crest Drive,
North Mankato, Minnesota 56003
www.capstonepub.com

Library of Congress
Cataloging-in-Publication Data
Cataloging-in-publication information is on file
with the Library of Congress.

ISBN 978-1-4795-8512-0 (hardcover)
ISBN 978-1-4795-8516-8 (paperback)
ISBN 978-1-4795-8520-5 (eBook PDF)

Written by Simon Holland

Printed in China
10 9 8 7 6 5 4 3 2 1

All photographs Shutterstock

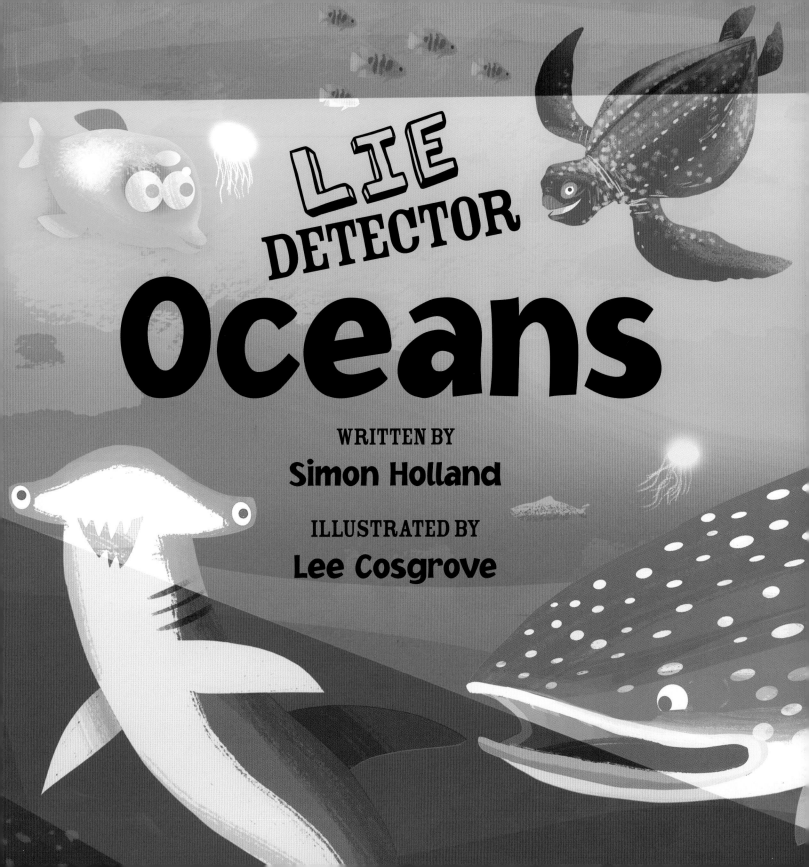

LIE
DETECTOR
Oceans

WRITTEN BY
Simon Holland

ILLUSTRATED BY
Lee Cosgrove

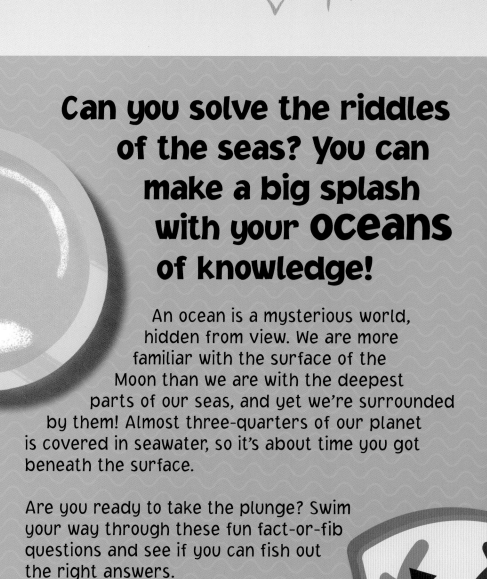

Can you solve the riddles of the seas? You can make a big splash with your OCEANS of knowledge!

An ocean is a mysterious world, hidden from view. We are more familiar with the surface of the Moon than we are with the deepest parts of our seas, and yet we're surrounded by them! Almost three-quarters of our planet is covered in seawater, so it's about time you got beneath the surface.

Are you ready to take the plunge? Swim your way through these fun fact-or-fib questions and see if you can fish out the right answers.

FIB!

Mudskippers are brainy fish that can breathe both in and out of the water. When they leave the water to search for food, they keep a mixture of air and water in their gills. They take in oxygen from the mixture, which keeps their bodies going perfectly.

Squish!

IN NO HURRY

Don't bet on this horse! With a top speed of 5 feet (1.52 meters) per hour, the dwarf seahorse is probably the slowest fish in the seas.

FACT!

Most speedboats zip across the surface of the sea at up to 62 miles (100 kilometers) per hour. But that's nothing compared to a sprinting black marlin. It's one of the world's fastest fish, clocking in at speeds of up to 81 miles (130 kilometers) per hour!

CREATURES OF HABIT

When it's time to build a nest and lay their eggs, most female sea turtles return to the same beach where they themselves hatched.

FIB!

Were you fooled? At 6 1/2 feet (2 m) long, and 1,433 pounds (650 kilograms), the leatherback is actually the largest living turtle on Earth. It's bigger than most adult humans! These gentle giants are named after their flexible, leather-like shells.

FACT!

Coral reefs are often called, the "rain forests of the sea." They are home to an incredible number of the world's plants and animals. For example, more than 4,000 different types of fish live on coral reefs.

Super Sleuth

The world's largest coral reef is the Great Barrier Reef, off the northeast coast of Australia. It stretches for more than 1,429 miles (2300 km) and can be seen by astronauts in orbit around the Earth.

FACT!

This shark has no need for toothpicks! The tiny pilot fish has come to eat the parasites from the shark's teeth and mouth. As payment for this clean-up job, the pilot fish is safe from other sea creatures. No one else dares to get this close!

Super Sleuth

This clown fish removes parasites from a giant sea anemone. In return, the stinging anemone keeps the fish safe from hungry attackers.

FIB!

Sharks do live in every ocean in the world, but they can also swim in rivers and lakes. They are able to survive in fresh (non-salty) water by peeing a lot! This helps them keep the right amount of salt in their bodies so that they can spend time in fresh water.

Yuck!

Super Sleuth

The speartooth shark (right) swims through freshwater rivers in northern Australia. But it makes trips to the ocean too.

FACT!

Every year gray whales leave their feeding areas in the Arctic. They head south to warmer waters in Mexico, but not on vacation! They go there to have their babies. By the time they return to the Arctic, some gray whales have completed a journey of up to 12,427 miles (20,000 kilometers).

FIB!

Marine iguanas live along the rocky coastlines of the Galapagos Islands in the Pacific Ocean. They look like monsters, but in fact they are gentle lizards that eat seaweed. They don't live in the sea, but the strongest and biggest of them can dive in and nibble the seaweed from rocks in deeper water.

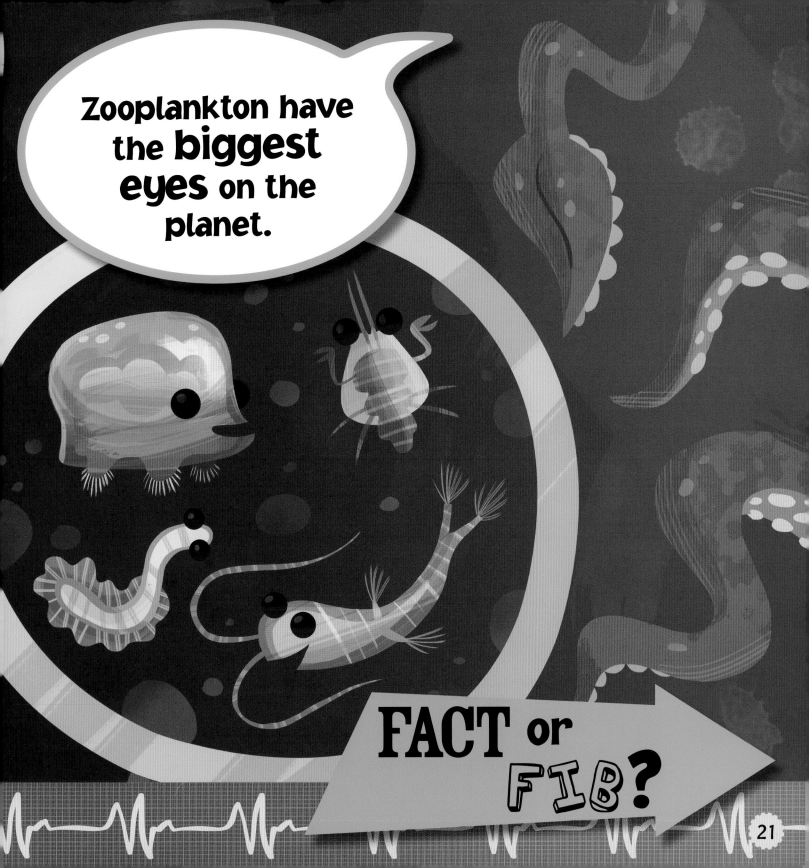

BEASTS OF THE DEEP

Giant squid live between 656 feet (220 kilometers) and 3,281 feet (1,000 kilometers) below the surface of the ocean. The largest one ever measured was 53 feet (16 m) long.

FIB!

Zooplankton are the smallest animals in the ocean. A zooplankton is smaller than the eraser on the end of your pencil. The giant squid holds the record for having the biggest eyes on Earth. At about 1 foot (30 centimeters) wide, its peepers are the size of dinner plates!

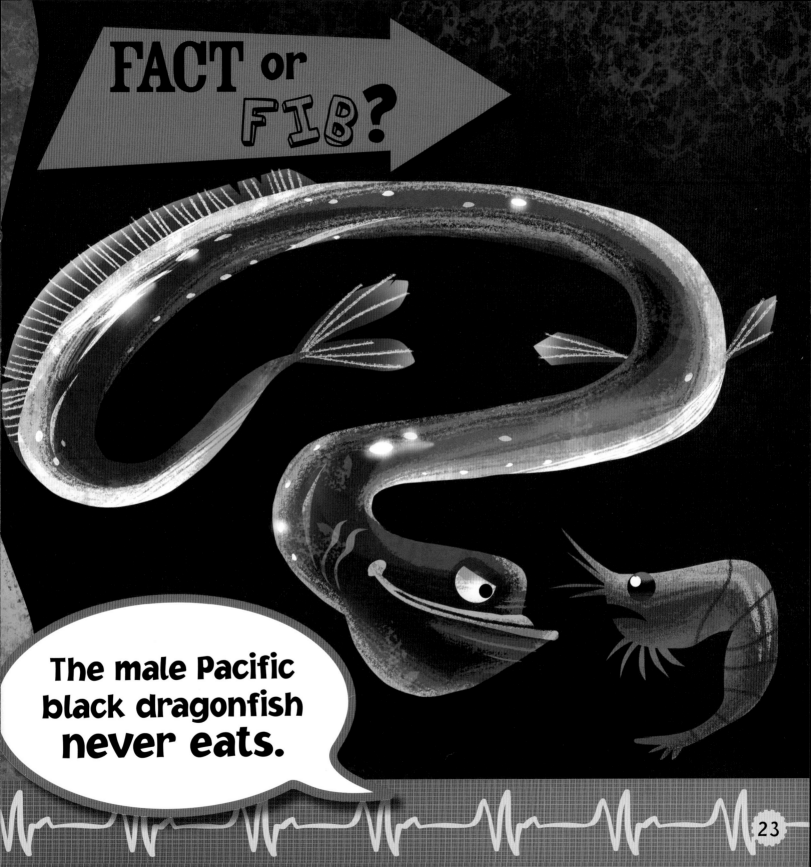

Super Sleuth

Female black dragonfish have a whisker-like lure on their lower jaw. They light up the lure to attract small sea animals for food.

Ha, ha!

FACT!

Female black dragonfish are hunters, and grow to 16 inches (41 cm) long. The males are much smaller, and they cannot eat food. They have no teeth, no stomach, and no digestive system. The males simply help the females have babies, and then they die.

FACT or FIB?

Penguins are a polar bear's favorite food.

NORTH POLE

FIB!

Polar bears and penguins live at opposite ends of the planet, and would never meet each other—except, perhaps, in a zoo. Polar bears live in the Arctic, at the top of the world, where they mainly hunt seals. Penguins live in Antarctica and South America, and in southern parts of South Africa and Australia.

I'm thinking of moving to the South Pole!

SOUTH POLE

Your journey of discovery continues ...

Congratulations! You've taken your first dip into the oceans, and you now know more than you did when you were standing on dry land. You've met some surprising fish, some animals living in unexpected places, and you've seen how dangerous predators can actually be gentle creatures. This book has also taken you to greater depths, where very few people have been. Now turn to the next page, where one final test lies in wait for you.

WHAT AND WHERE?

How well do you remember the creatures you met when you made your journey through the oceans? Here's a challenge to test you. Take a look at these pictures and see if you can answer the questions correctly. You get bonus points if you can remember an extra fact about each animal or place in the pictures!

2. Can you name this big lizard?

1. What is this animal home called?

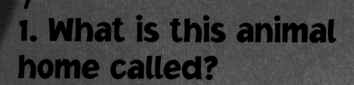

3. What kind of fish is this?

5. Which creature owns these teeth?

4. Where does this animal live?

CHOOSE YOUR ANSWERS FROM THE OPTIONS HERE:

A. Arctic
B. Coral reef
C. Shark
D. Marine iguana
E. Mudskipper

Answers: 1. B, 2. D, 3. E, 4. A, 5. C.

GLOSSARY

coral reef—an area of hard, stony structures, called corals, which form in shallow seas

digestive system—the parts of the body that process food, to create energy for an animal

gills—the parts of an animal that take in oxygen from water

mangrove forest—a type of forest that grows along muddy shores in warm, tropical regions

oxygen—a gas that animals take in, through breathing, to keep their bodies working well

parasite—a very small living thing that lives inside or on another living thing

predator—an animal that hunts and eats other animals

sea anemone—a flower-like creature with venom-filled, stinging tentacles

submarine—a vehicle that can take people deep underwater

zooplankton—tiny, floating animals.

Fishinating!

INDEX